this alaska

this alaska

carlie hoffman

four way books
tribeca

Library of Congress Cataloging-in-Publication Data

Names: Hoffman, Carlie, author.
Title: This Alaska / Carlie Hoffman.
Description: New York, New York : Four Way Books, [2021]
Identifiers: LCCN 2021005295 | ISBN 9781945588921 (paperback)
Subjects: LCGFT: Poetry.
Classification: LCC PS3608.O47753 T48 2021 | DDC 811/.6--dc23
LC record available at https://lccn.loc.gov/2021005295

This book is manufactured in the United States of America and printed on
acid-free paper.

Four Way Books is a not-for-profit literary press. We are grateful for the assistance
we receive from individual donors, public arts agencies, and private foundations.

This publication is made possible with public funds from the
National Endowment for the Arts

and from the New York State Council on the Arts, a state agency,

PROUD MEMBER

[clmp]

We are a proud member of the Community of Literary Magazines and Presses.

contents

I

II

III

It was the love which the hunter has for living things, and which he can only express by aiming his gun at them.

—Italo Calvino

Learning to be still

All afternoon it rains on the traffic
outside my window. It's nothing new,
but I can't get the thought of pigeons,
strange magistrates of sickness and beauty,
carved away from me, or how it's been two years
since I've stood in a line of waitresses
at the hot-food window of a restaurant
in Hackensack, New Jersey, the row of us
identical in black slacks and kitchen shoes,
like pigeons stacked along a telephone wire, waiting
to serve fish and curry rice to strangers.
I was so young before New York that I believed
loving myself each day
would be easier there. But lying
in bed, I can hear the wind, and the trees shaking
because they have no choice,
and I want to go someplace where the trees grow apples
shiny and persistent as stars. Of course it hurts
knowing how wrong this is, this constant need
for movement, even backwards, like my desire,
just now, to enter the bathroom
of some North Jersey diner after
licking the gravy bowl clean,
after so much hunger, and return to the dinner rush

wearing an apron again, coffee pot in hand,
to walk in circles until there becomes
no here or now to speak of.

aLaska

For weeks I've envisioned an iceberg
on the cusp of breakage. A north star stitched
overhead, calling.

My sisters stand framed
in black ribbon, pretty
as two distant hills.

Eleven barefoot summers we scanned
the wharf for snowshoe hares,
watched gulls cut through wind

in reckless vicissitude.
One night I dreamed I was
a caught mermaid netted

inside a ship's hull. Another,
the three of us cast
in an emergency of waves,

woken just before the drowning.
I learned how not
to be the vanished sister.

To suck meat from crab legs,
peel out the eyes for otters,
place the shells carefully

into the yellow bucket.
To speak as though nothing
and everything were crucial,

as though the wish for two souls
like gulls returning to rock
were possible, night workers swarming

the dock, reeking of fishwater.

I DON'T ALWAYS TELL THE TRUTH

Believe me when I tell you
our visions have lost

all meaning. This morning one came
like a stone dropped to the bottom

of a well. The solution for lightlessness
is going down there. To climb

into the dark like you know
what you are looking for.

In the same way I have forgotten
entire people, I am just now learning

the names for the furniture
that separates us. Sometimes sleep

is wicked; sometimes it's a sparrow
driving its beak in dirt.

ςoat

For six years we slept in a porcelain tub.
The door bolted, mother smoking
quietly at the window, faucet run high
to bleach my father's return from the night.
The seventh year, the year he came home
in late afternoon, carrying a severed goat's
head, he was done, he said, finished
with the milk and pills of other women,
and nailed it to the wall in the living room.

WITHOUT CENTRIFUGE

In the middle of the night my sisters dig out
the pale birds graphed along the waterside
and fix them to a willow.

Relax, they say, *it only gets worse.*
Last season's nests collapse
beneath our palms, as we kneel for the angel

who bargained his way to Anchorage, exploded
the moment he landed, and became a gull
rounding the wharf like a conjurer.

soLstIce

Tonight winter lays its cold hand on your forehead, and the valley rinses white with snow. You swear, finally, you could sleep through April. You could sleep, if only the grackle at the window stopped tapping her hard beak to glass. The slow sheet of her body brief, shining color against the dark. What the pines once were before snowfall. It's the smallest noises, you remember, that carry deep loss. Like a key splashing into a pond. The grackle calls from the ledge, her song dim and precise as a bell, and you begin to suck on an ending that makes most sense: You as a boy running errands with your mother. Your red gloves. The silver bell above the butcher's front door, the butcher who loved your hair. Sometimes he'd give you sausage dangling from a thin, white string. This kept you happy, you decide, kept you still, the boar staring down from the hook. At your window the winter sky turns silver, turns away, and it occurs to you, now, in this moment, how you never thought about its heart. You assumed, no—believed, the heart lives. That one day it will eat its way out and sing.

DISSOCIATION

We traveled northwest
of our intelligence, the lighthouse
whipping its beam
across our backs.

The ferryman
tossed us a lit match
and said
see for yourself.

What we carried:
violet rooms
that tucked themselves
into more
violet rooms, our mouths
stupid in
surveillance of
the marmot-scattered hills.

There is something in us
that needs
our ghosts to lift from
our chests so things
get colder and more free.

I am not
colder and more free

but here the wild
kneels down in me.
When the prayer bell calls,
we walk
along the shore path,
water laps
into the bay.
There are stars.

The steady creak
of a bow. The moon, a swan's
neck without its corpse.

WINteR

When my sisters can't scrub the oil
from the sick gull's feathers, they clip

its wings, untie the cord that binds
the slow sheet of its body

and plant it into a wooden box
drilled with tiny holes. It is my turn

to bring the diseased bird
to the breeder across the bank:

his medicine knives, his hut occupied
with feeders and soap. But because I am

youngest, because a hunter's moon
is how I locate heaven, I take the gull

down the wharf, kneel in an untouched
tract of snow, and quiet its skull with rock.

HUNTING Lesson

In the lozenge-colored glow of the garage
you are the hero skinning a rabbit

bit by bit, careful not to hook a vein.
I am the daughter peering through the window.

What if the world really is a stale bowl of water
that we can't keep our fingers out of—

The night sky stiffens in a squeal of light.
How can I look away?

WISHBONE

When the butcher at the grocery gives you
the brittle symmetry, you do not, at first, think it's a
mistake as you ask him for another, hold both thin
ends between each of your index fingers, then
slowly pull, to show your daughter how it works.
Instead, you remember your first Thanksgiving
without a father. A smaller turkey browning in a pan
through oven light, your mother's blue dress, you
perched on the counter with your eyes shut, the wish
quietly forming on your tongue.

You look at your daughter, her brown eyes closed,
waiting for you to begin the count, and as the butcher
wraps the sliced meat in wax paper, you suddenly
realize it wasn't your mother drawing
the thinner half that made it unfavorable.
It was how, when you opened up your eyes again
to the empty space at the kitchen table,
everything around you grew heavier, and now you want
to take back what you've done, for your small daughter
standing patiently in front of you to remain living
within the perfect, watery second before
she re-enters the world. Though this wish
is useless, too, because she has already seen

the bruised, discolored edges, the dried blood
near the top, because she has held it in her hand
and touched it, and you have already
described to her, by example,
the way things will end.

Now you are certain, more than ever,
of what comes next: There is no
clean break, not with the way we must always
lean against one another, for definition,
and how the ending has nothing to do
with going back to being half again, but rather
split jaggedly, the end is everything
about the particular lie that makes us capable
of believing ourselves whole.

DISPOSING the animal

It was winter. You placed your gloves
on the chair near the fire. The lake
was already frozen, already the sound
of skaters breached the window.

Through cottonwood you could
see their shadows twist
across the ice—sometimes
falling, sometimes waiting to get up.

I, too, have seen my shadow
and wanted to travel through it.

In the dream
I lie down in snow, a bullet
pearled in the shell of my palm,
a hand in the other, so I might feel
both kinds of sacrifice.

CONTINUUM

My mother split each day open
like a gutted fish. Her hours, a tarp
draped over a stranger's head.
The way grief works:

a mirror the chemical
that ruins the body,
a window, a small blue prayer
gone missing.

In a kitchen far away, I draw
my mother's mouth.

It's hard not to remember certain people
as a ghost-house caught
in a storm of lilac.
It's hard not to want
to be remembered.

Through the corner of the window
a shock of jays tilt their beaks in sun
then go on in warm oblivion.

If I go on, it is the story of a turquoise girl
crossing a meadow. I press my tongue
on the peach of her shoulder.

If there is reason
to be human, this
is its search ground—
light pulled apart as a trout's spine.
When she speaks she is no one you knew.

after BURIAL

In the music box a wooden angel spins,
making her own weather.

Near the riverbank where we
buried the gulls, I light a candle

and wait, patient as a hunter detecting
what the wind will do

in foliage. Someone,
somewhere, will see it.

The flame glowing like a toy sun
or a trick God.

If we did not go back
we'd be kinder.

The wind forces the fire out
and I leave only to return

to this river where the gulls
rise, small white banshees

oiled in music.

II

tHere is no doubt you are Hemmed in by something not yet fixed

Bird by bird, June surrounds the hospital.

When they took me, I chose
to be taken, my stereo
sharpened with bees.

Thirst announced itself like a tulip
pinned to the bottom
of my throat.

All winter I starved myself
to make room for God, the birds

balanced on a crutch of cedar.
Wind shook the trees to flee them.

aLaska

Everyone darkened by Alaska,
crooked with the weight of marmots

and wild-haired children who chase them,
sticks held by pink, slender fingers.

The small engines of their bodies
caged with laughter, glinting.

The scene struck by a carnival danger
no one speaks of.

In dreams the dead
come into houses. Always

at random and the way we imagine:
bringing the wind with their gold raincoats.

We want to wash their faces
in sunlight, they want us to show them

what they smelled like.
I can't tell you the invention that makes light

fold out of the room when they enter,
but it's called Alaska, glacial,

possessed by night.
In childhood I believed so carelessly

I'd kneel in the backyard, brittle December,
palms against dirt in prayer, careless

as the rooms children vanish to
when we forget to look.

bloemenmarkt

Each time I meet with God
he is still singing and jealous
of the way I've learned to speak
with my hands. By autumn
I am drunk in the bathtub again.
The water is warm. I think of December
and the Christmas trees sold
along the Singel, the flower market
brimming with black coats.
Like pine, I am desperate to be lit.
God tells me I am embarrassing
at love. I tell him he is lucky—
all mighty, but all voice.

ORION

In my dream the dead have arrived
as escorts. We travel

past cold hills and wolves
wild in a deadlocked field. A corporation

of stars cracks overhead. I lean
my hand where the hunting dogs

chase the rabbit, and they tell me
constellation means assembled

for life. Then they lend me
a shovel and dissolve into night.

There is no other way back. I dig
through snow until the cold metal strikes.

exoskeLetoN

We grow sick of the prayers we
knife into our thighs, as a small

stranded girl with a crow in her arms
is pilgrimming, her head

crowned with the rookery.
We seal each window, unbutton

our shirts and scrape a map to the river
beneath our breasts. We cannot wait

for rapture, or the betrayal
of light to restore the fields.

We parcel a sack of belongings,
set fire to the house, and speak

of a hunter licking salt
from a speared wolf's paw.

WHY I MOVED TO NEW YORK

There are so many lunatics in this city and sometimes
I am one of them, forgetting, walking out
into the evening wind, its sky of three bleak stars.
I go out without washing my hair, away from my small
rented room with its one cracked wall
mosaicked in taped-on postcards from cities
much more elegant and clean
than I have ever been. I am lying.
I do not forget nearly anything
and so many lovers ago it was spring.
I lived in a town in Jersey named
for its neatly cut grass. It's true
I thought a lot about dying as I drove each morning
to buy gas station coffee. I have never told this
to anyone. Instead, after waitressing the dinner shift
I would go to my favorite bar
and order beer. I would lie down drunk
in the grass looking up
at all those tiny bursts of bright dead light
and learn a different form for surrender.

after the need to keep other worlds

We wait for night to return
to the river, our hands now cold and capable

carrying the shovels. Our feet
dampened with reeds. In new light

the sunk gulls surface, pale beaks
turned upward like teeth. Already

the evidence disassembles. I ask what happens
after the need to keep other worlds

at their distances, each with their own
cruel sun to kneel beneath.

We search wet ground for evenness, we dig
the graves to bury the stiff, white birds

along the riverbank, turn away from them.
Beside a thicket, a pair of whitetails

fold their bodies on the cusp
of sleep, infant antlers

darkened by cloud. To kill
is unremarkable. Who lied to you.

to brooklyn and part way back

When I couldn't make you love
winter I spent a lot of time underground,
riding the C train from my uptown station
down to the last stop at Euclid,
and though I disliked Brooklyn for its
other-worldness and so-far-awayness, I
liked all the different colored shoes I'd see
from stop to stop, and how the bars
hang Christmas lights year round. I tried—
packing snow in the freezer to make
things casual, and later the air conditioner
always on until the only option left
was touch, but just like thinking God
could show up in a creek styled as the heron
we followed last June, through stone and sledge
to the swimming hole, our naked backs
riddled with sun like kaleidoscopes, it was useless
wanting to perfect change
and so inexact as truth. What matters
is what we tell each other for certain:
Winter is coming. I bet my life on this.

SUDDEN HYMN IN WINTER

Some women are all the women
you've ever loved at once. Somewhere else
a man chases her image with a can
of orange spray paint. Evening has already
happened. He shades the almost
touching, half-formed hands of Matisse's dancers
onto the side of the train, and her light
is different now, though he knows this isn't possible,
not really. Light does not change, just gets lost
inside the greater thing. And if he could go back
it wouldn't be to the hospital
where the sun forked through the space
his body left as he turned out of the room,
or the first kiss, but farther still, to the moment
just before, looking out at the pond in muzzled
autumn, the fish curving on the cusp
of emergency, all those rivers mapped inside them.
And they'd watch quietly until sundown,
because he doesn't do this work for forgiveness,
but because the fact of grace
disgusts him.

He knows this much:
It was winter. Her hair was thinning. After,
for a while, it is winter all the time.

RIDING HOME ON THE 1 TRAIN at 5 am

Just now a woman in a yellow
dress and matching hair bands enters the train
holding a plastic microphone,
and, because at midnight she turned fifty-two,
will sing *Happy Birthday* through the eleven
screeching stops home. *Happy birthday to me*
she is stomping her suede purple heel
as she sways from one end of the car
to the other. *Happy, happy*
birthday, even in the elevator as I
make my way toward the subway exit, her metal cane
tapping against cement like a drumstick.
I don't know if she is drunk on gin or some other
almost upper that slowly ends in disgust,
though that is not my story to tell.
Somehow it is autumn. Somehow, yesterday,
I managed to wash my sheets. Like you,
I do not know if happiness
is anything more extravagant than a goal
to shape our lives toward, and it's
too early for the rest of our lives.

MIDNIGHT SUN

When the dawn gulls call
we meet them near the wharf's edge.

There is wind. The ferryman
gone, quarters scattered

along the dock. The sun a rusted
knob unhounding light.

Our landscape: blond hills stretch
into more blond hills. Our tongues

stunned in observance of whitetails
in the field. Everywhere, unflinching, the public

glare of August. Never have we been
so involved with our bodies, the risk

of them. A sorrow soft
and punctual as antlers in bloom.

mime in anchorage station

There is nothing I can tell you about your death
without my hands. My mouth, swollen
with black leaves.

In the creases of my palms: news of a bridge
useful as a weapon, then prayer, then

a story where someone does not come
home holding flowers, does not pour
milk in the cat's metal dish.

My hands are capable of chalk
and the failure

of love to deliver us back
to where dark is good.

I hold a candle to your face, listen.

anniversary

The girl stands on a street corner facing the high school.
It is Sunday, but out front a custodian uses a wooden broom

to clear the fallen leaves into trash bags.
She could have gone anywhere.

To the church, an empty field, to the overpass
near the school, but instead she chose here,

late November, wearing her black coat,
a rose from the city in her hand.

Today, eight years ago, she must have been
doing something important,

but she can't quite remember what.
Waiting in line with her mother at the market

to purchase the last good apples
of autumn, or staring in a mirror at the plaza

while getting a haircut.
She watches in the cold as the old man knots

shut the top of a filled bag, then makes his way
from the far end of the street, inward.

She can't help but desire to hate him,
his cut knuckles, his cheeks

fevered from the song of working quickly against wind.
She hates him for not pausing

to see her, for the decades of furniture
that separate them, for doing wrong by sleep.

He keeps on sweeping the leaves into blond piles
like dead hair on a barber's floor, not looking up

at the girl, the scrap of town, the detail of snow
beginning in the branches.

This is the only lesson: Without darkness
there is no music. Through December

she will pray hard beside the window,
toward the ancient trees, people drifting by

out of habit, out of getting on,
the foreign hum of bootsteps.

A prayer that someday she can use this,
that somehow, in the middle, she will wake

styled in the fire and wet light
of winter stars, deciding to begin.

BEYOND THE FIELD

I stood in the center
while the blizzard
went on and on. A snowshoe hare
curled near a perimeter of pine
like a closed white hand,
and I knew that soon this snow
would erase me. Impermanence
is the first way of knowing the world,
the second, a love of it regardless.
Beyond the field there are hills,
though it was too dark to see.
There is a pond where a tern tests the quickness
of water's weight to anchor him.

The dead press the old light of their fingers
along the land-tract of our skin.
They tell us it is terrible
the way we brighten as we move on.

III

postcarᴅ fʀom aLaska

The clouds above Barrow swell.
Blackbirds squat among telephone wires

like stoics, and I have forgotten
the procedure of prayer. My hands

still my hands, the shape they make so my mouth
warms them. Interchangeable to the scene

where I hold a half-dead gull, oil already
corroding its nerves. Parts of its skull
no longer light up.

People, too, contain a dangerous spill
inside them: a transmitter out
of date, whole spheres submerged

in serotonin. If I can believe
in electricity, I can believe the dead
still live somewhere—

a zip code to a dim, immutable
breathing. A voice calling out
This is not the body you longed for—

Even the crows who stalk power
lines have flown from someplace else.

as for me, i used to be a bird

I'm trying to convince you I am less lunatic now
so each afternoon on my smoke break I count
the pigeons shimmying between the buildings
studding Lexington Avenue
until I've traveled back to the creek
where we witnessed the first heron of my life.
She was so blue and big and saintlike
and out of our reach, already dissolving beak first
into summer's impossible heat. It hurt
going after her and it was nuts, too, going on
toward something we had no business
looking into, no answer to respond with
if she asked her only question: *What is your intention here?*
Which is also, like all premonition, a kind of prayer:
Inside this creek, the saints will be all blue.
Three months from here, you
will be as far away without vanishing
as the heron, as the pigeons now rummaging
the gutter while I ash my cigarette onto the curb. I cannot
keep track of their numbers, cannot imagine the end
of my obsession with bleeding one lost thing
into another. The pigeons
are a mess of black, white, grey, and umber.

They are saying *Here is your life.*
Why do you refuse to show up?

SUDDEN HYMN IN AUGUST

Everyone's asleep besides the lovers
who have just returned from the Jeep's backseat,
shivering with rain. Not wanting night to end yet,
they grab a bottle of gin leftover in the mini fridge
and tiptoe toward the balcony, careful
not to wake the dark figures snoring gently
on the rug. By now they've already drunk
enough beer to restlessly consider the amount of stars
it would take to chart the shape of West Virginia,
that yellow-blurred state he will leave her for,
though neither of them knows this.
They are young enough to believe
that stars and sex are the terms of salvation.
It's raining heavier and for a long time they sit in plastic chairs
overlooking the small, rectangular slab of motel pool,
observing the thick drops dissolve inside it.
Perhaps this is why they came here in the first place:
some inherent longing for a windful of salt
and the ocean that is never quite done with itself.
And they don't need to be finished either
not with the rain that is blowing onto them, too,
hitting the roof like a pile of the evening's cans

dumped into the trash. They don't have to agree
there is something spectacular or whole that is coming
from any of this, only that they are here.

DISOBEDIENCE

In a city reined by nothing but the locusts'
white smoke and streets of cable

littered with crows,
winter bites our necks.

A spire punctures the sky
like the horn of a bull

charged deep through a man's chest.
Behind the church, a drained fountain

the color of a father gone cold again.
Inside it: a crow calls and calls.

Is it forgiveness he wants?
Because I am good

I reach my hands in the fountain.
I lift the crow by his throat.

scene at the central park zoo, Late winter

This morning, we are two of a handful of people
stuttering through the zoo. No work today
because we skipped it and wandered here,
where drizzle falls on and off onto leftover snow.
Three macaques bend toward us
and shove their leather-tipped fingers
through the metal wiring to grab hold
of the orange slices I've peeled for them.
Frenzied, the small creatures, slightly human,
struggle for my hand. I recognize their appetite,
though it shames me—the devouring
of something foreign and sweet
cutting through the circumstance of a life.
February 8th, 2016. Lunar New Year
and the Year of the Monkey,
year of the intelligence to stop asking why.
When my palms are finally empty, we turn
toward our fragment of the gate.
Newly divorced, you toss the puzzle of orange peels
into the trash and motion for the exit.
Suddenly, I know this is why you were angry
last night when, after we slept together,

I asked for the takeout we'd saved in the fridge.

Above us, a downpour designs itself in the clouds.

I tell you none of what I know until now.

NORtH WINDOW

On any given day two people are building a room, wishing it becomes a cathedral. Together, they choose the white curtains to hang from the rod of their bedside window. Spring mud comes up through sidewalk cracks. The mango sun makes the street of brick apartments shine the color of a lion's back. The distant clouds. They paint the frame the muddy, tin shade of sycamore bark. The walls: the fleshy underbelly of a fish. An illusion of breathing dizzily under water, like peering through a cathedral's stained glass. It was like lions, they want to say, but can't. Instead, while they work, they consider all the clouds in the corners of all the windows of their pasts: a school bus, a sliding screen door at the threshold of a den. Always looking out, distracted, and thinking about sex. And once, the December morning spent staring up in Rembrandtplein Square, watching the clouds rush over the tops of spires. The clouds like sudden lions blazing across a clear and steady plain, flooded with light. They told themselves the Earth was spinning away beneath their feet. First, because they didn't know what it felt like. After, because they did.

HISTORY

The summer before,
we found an otter dried up on the wharf.

You scoured its oiled fur
with the tip

of a kitchen match, the eyes already
picked clean by gulls.

Don't look, which meant
all I could have done was watch you

as you lifted the dark carcass
into a trash can. *Light it*,

which meant *Stay*
until the sun orphaned the landscape

and we stood in the dangerous glow
of the sun we'd made.

WHILe waitinɡ in Line at Lenox fish market, i imaɡine somepLace eLse

Today it's tilapia. Tomorrow, trout.
One by one she lifts them from buckets
night fishermen brought from Genoa, and even
after she rinses each one separately, peels
scum and dirt from the skin,
they will still keep that same bewildered expression
on their faces as she positions their forms in ice.
What happens in death is tall
and far away as childhood.
She does it with the weighted hands
of a mortician patting blush
on the cheeks of the dead. Imagine
the creatures knocking like spoons
beneath the Mediterranean,
their whole school a silver light
darkened by nets. Before
the motorcycle, the accident, gasoline and his
face scalped back along the Riviera,
the lemon trees blond with August.

THe WomeN of HIGHBRIDGe paRK

It's noon on Sunday and they gather
around black milk crates placed in a circle
on tattered blue fishing tarp. It's not quite
March, but it's one of those fluke
hot-weather days, and they are so prepared
for spring: swapping old records
packed in cardboard cartons,
daisies tucked behind their ears,
gossiping in the kind of Spanish
from the kitchens of my past. Last night
at the bar in a flurry of bitterness
I chucked my full beer
at the bathroom wall, then walked
the thirty blocks home. Today
I am thinking about the significance
of grass and how I came here because I want
to get better at being a person,
but every day I begin to know less
about who I am to America. All I know
is a small girl emerges from the trees
waving a stick, hollers to her mother
that the large scrap of rock she's been resting on
is lake water, bottle shards scattered
across its surface like glittering

jagged pieces of a life.
I have been trying more each year
to be comfortable, and maybe
a little bit proud of how I've learned
to make a home, all this daylight
kicking toward the lawn to give
what little it owes.

NIGHt DRIVE WItH mY BROtHeR tHROUGH WARWICK vaLLey

It's winter again and can you blame me for feeling
how little our wills matter, how tonight
even though the weather app alerts us of a storm
we drive in my used Civic with its shot brake lights
two hours north through Warwick, New York,
snow already frosted on the phone wires,
just so we can lie down shivering in a field
and look at stars, and despite the blizzard
piling like a hive surrounding the diner
where we wind up forced
to stick it out all night, we agree
over burnt coffee and gravy fries
that this is the place we needed
to get to for a while. And for a while
we talk music and Orpheus and how
his perfect mistake was thinking that the point
was as long as he played, even the grass
would always love him back.
To believe in the unconditional, you say,
is wrong. I'd like to correct you
but I catch a glimpse of your shaved chin in the booth's
harsh light and remember the morning you knocked
on the bathroom door with your eyes low, a razor
in your hand, asking me to show you how.

This was the spring right after our father, strung out
and alone with you, called you *faggot*,
and what came next could not have been music
because even though you were finally tall enough
to throw it back, by the time I sped home from
another double shift at the bar
the cops had dragged you away.
Brother, what you really want to tell me is, *Let it go*,
because our father is dying and that is why
I came home this Christmas, even though
we haven't talked in years. Hours before
I drove to the drug store to pick up the script, returned
to the house I have fled from, and silently fed him his pills.
It is true that, on our best days, music out-survives us,
but mostly, like Orpheus milk-deep in the after-image
of his turning back, it is everything we've ever given up.

pact

It's not my business, but each time I glimpse
a small girl, bleary-eyed, staring down
at her shoes, hair greased
from longing as the train
rattles on over rats and bits of trash
through the dark, I want
to make a girl-pact
that whatever she is
dreaming there, night flashing
at her back, she will go on
in spite of. Though it is not
my business just
a moment ago you stood
four-feet tall on the subway stairs,
the railing between them:
I'll fucking smack you
Fuck you bitch
as you tried to pull
your mother's coat
away from the years of what
comes next. Not
my business, but know
this is not about the story of a
mother and father gone bad, but worse—

it is about a woman and man
alone, so many houses ago,
picking dog hair from the meat
chucked on the living room rug,
thick in the part of the plot
of your inheritance, and as you walk
up the stairs toward the tail end
of winter, a twist to your pace,
I can only give you this pact:
When you grow taller and repulsed
by your hair pinned back, the tie
around your neck while you carry
hot plates from table to table, your heart
a half-stone tugging you inward, when your
rage for the order of things shocks you
into stillness, move faster
until you reach a room in a city
you recognize least, and you will
know to call this home.

OVERNIGHT

The orchard rinses white with tiny bones
until there is nothing left but a wish

to drag out mice curled deep in the tunnels
and string them from a sycamore.

Tonight the young empty themselves
in a football field, behind bleachers—

their beautiful hands, ribs glossed by
stadium light, then, slowly, as if still

searching for something not there, return
to the starry oval of their beds.

Who are we if not images
that betray us? The street is quiet.

Snow begins in the leaves.

Grateful acknowledgement is made to the editors of the following publications
in which these poems, sometimes in different forms, first appeared:
*Angime, Bennington Review, Boston Review, Canary: A Literary Journal of the
Environmental Crisis, Chicago Quarterly Review, Cider Press Review,
Conjunctions, The Cortland Review, Elke: A Little Journal, The Florida Review,
Gulf Stream Literary Magazine, The Harvard Advocate, Jai-Alai Magazine,
The Los Angeles Review, Meridian, Narrative Magazine, Nashville Review,
The New England Review, Nimrod International Journal, Ninth Letter,
Poet's Country, Supporting Women Writers in Miami (SWWIM),
The Texas Review, TriQuarterly, THRUSH, Two Peach,* and *WomenArts
Quarterly Journal.*

Thank you to everyone at Four Way Books, particularly Martha Rhodes, Ryan
Murphy, and Clarissa Long for believing in this book. My deepest gratitude.

For fellowships to sustain my writing and study poetry, thank you to:
Columbia University's School of the Arts Writing Program, the New York
State Summer Writers Institute at Skidmore College, and the Juniper
Summer Writing Institute at UMass Amherst. I am profoundly thankful for
the support.

Thank you to my teachers, in all iterations: Josh Bell, Peg Boyers,
Lucie Brock-Broido, Henri Cole, Cynthia Cruz, Timothy Donnelly,
Michael Dumanis, Monica Ferrell, Emily Fragos, Carolyn Forché,
Alan Gilbert, James Hoch, Binnie Kirshenbaum, Ada Limón,
Campbell McGrath, Lynn Melnick, Rob Ostrom, Geoffrey Sadock,
Nicholas Samaras, Maggie Smith, Lynne Sharon Schwartz,

William Wadsworth, Rosanna Warren, and Alan Ziegler. Your dedication and love of language continues to shape and incite my own.

I am deeply grateful for the close readings and friendships of: Marci Calabretta Cancio-Bello, Meghan Maguire Dahn, Michelle Delaney, Ariel Francisco, Matthew Gellman, Jordan Hewson, Devin Kelly, Dan Kraines, Erin Lynn, Nadra Mabrouk, Elizabeth Metzger, Nicolas Millan, Carly Joy Miller, Catherine Pond, JV Portella, Richard Quigley, Max Ritvo, Hannah Starr Rogers, Colin Ryan, Megan Walsh, and Anna Rose Welch. Thank you to The Many Louise Glücks and my cohort at Columbia. Thank you to LBB's thesis workshop: Baba Badji, Zeeshan Pathan, Gnaomi Siemens, Frank Virgintino, and David Wallace. "Mime in Anchorage Station" is for Nicholas Arnoldi. A special thank you to Johnny Steers.

Thank you to my mother, Barbara Hoffman, always.

Carlie Hoffman is a poet and translator from New Jersey. Her honors include a 92Y Discovery Prize and a *Poets & Writers* Amy Award. She is the founder and editor-in-chief of *Small Orange Journal*. *This Alaska* is her first book. She lives in New York City.

Publication of this book was made possible by grants and donations. We are also grateful to those individuals who participated in our 2020 Build a Book Program. They are:

Anonymous (14), Robert Abrams, Nancy Allen, Maggie Anderson, Sally Ball, Matt Bell, Laurel Blossom, Adam Bohannon, Lee Briccetti, Therese Broderick, Jane Martha Brox, Christopher Bursk, Liam Callanan, Anthony Cappo, Carla & Steven Carlson, Paul & Brandy Carlson, Renee Carlson, Cyrus Cassells, Robin Rosen Chang, Jaye Chen, Edward W. Clark, Andrea Cohen, Ellen Cosgrove, Peter Coyote, Janet S. Crossen, Kim & David Daniels, Brian Komei Dempster, Matthew DeNichilo, Carl Dennis, Patrick Donnelly, Charles Douthat, Morgan Driscoll, Lynn Emanuel, Monica Ferrell, Elliot Figman, Laura Fjeld, Michael Foran, Jennifer Franklin, Sarah Freligh, Helen Fremont & Donna Thagard, Reginald Gibbons, Jean & Jay Glassman, Ginny Gordon, Lauri Grossman, Naomi Guttman & Jonathan Mead, Mark Halliday, Beth Harrison, Jeffrey Harrison, Page Hill Starzinger, Deming Holleran, Joan Houlihan, Thomas & Autumn Howard, Elizabeth Jackson, Christopher Johanson, Voki Kalfayan, Maeve Kinkead, David Lee, Jen Levitt, Howard Levy, Owen Lewis, Jennifer Litt, Sara London & Dean Albarelli, David Long, James Longenbach, Excelsior Love, Ralph & Mary Ann Lowen, Jacquelyn Malone, Donna Masini, Catherine McArthur, Nathan McClain, Richard McCormick, Victoria McCoy, Ellen McCulloch-Lovell, Judith McGrath, Debbie & Steve Modzelewski, Rajiv Mohabir, James T. F. Moore, Beth Morris, John Murillo & Nicole Sealey, Michael & Nancy Murphy, Maria Nazos, Kimberly Nunes, Bill O'Brien, Susan Okie & Walter Weiss, Rebecca Okrent, Sam Perkins, Megan Pinto, Kyle Potvin, Glen Pourciau, Kevin Prufer, Barbara Ras, Victoria Redel, Martha Rhodes, Paula Rhodes, Paula Ristuccia, George & Nancy Rosenfeld, M. L. Samios, Peter & Jill Schireson, Rob Schlegel, Roni & Richard Schotter, Jane Scovell, Andrew Seligsohn & Martina Anderson, James & Nancy Shalek, Soraya Shalforoosh, Peggy Shinner, Dara-Lyn Shrager, Joan Silber, Emily Sinclair, James Snyder & Krista Fragos, Alice St. Claire-Long, Megan Staffel, Bonnie Stetson, Yerra Sugarman, Dorothy Tapper Goldman, Marjorie & Lew Tesser, Earl Teteak, Parker & Phyllis Towle, Pauline Uchmanowicz, Rosalynde Vas Dias, Connie Voisine, Valerie Wallace, Doris Warriner, Ellen Doré Watson, Martha Webster & Robert Fuentes, Calvin Wei, Bill Wenthe, Allison Benis White, Michelle Whittaker, and Ira Zapin.